SUSIE'S Aquarium

The author and publishers are grateful to
Mr Andrew Grant, Vet M.B., M.R.C.V.S., for his
advice during the preparation of this book.

British Library Cataloguing in Publication Data

Snell, Nigel
  Susie's aquarium.
  1.Aquarium. Fish. Care
  I. Title   II. Series
  639.3'4
  ISBN 0–340–50021–2

Text and illustrations copyright © Nigel Snell 1989

First published in 1989

All rights reserved. No part of this publication may be
reproduced or transmitted in any form or by any means,
electronically or mechanically, including photocopying,
recording, or any information storage and retrieval system,
without either prior permission in writing from
the publisher or a licence permitting restricted copying.
In the United Kingdom such licences are issued by the
Copyright Licensing Agency, 33–34 Alfred Place,
London WC1B 3DP.

Published by Hodder and Stoughton Children's Books,
a division of Hodder and Stoughton Ltd,
Mill Road, Dunton Green, Sevenoaks, Kent TN13 2YA

Printed in Belgium by Proost International Book Production

A FIRST  BOOK

SUSIE'S Aquarium

BY NIGEL SNELL

HODDER AND STOUGHTON
LONDON SYDNEY AUCKLAND TORONTO

An unexpected pet

Susie has won a goldfish at the fair. She carries it home in a plastic bag filled with water.
'Poor little fish,' says Susie. 'There's hardly any room for you to swim.'

Daddy fetches a big mixing bowl and fills it with water. He opens the plastic bag and slowly lowers it into the water. He lets it float until the temperature of the water inside the bag feels the same as the water outside. Then he empties the goldfish into the bowl.

'Tomorrow we'll go and buy an aquarium,' says Daddy. 'Your goldfish will be much happier in a proper tank.'

Buying the aquarium

The next morning Susie and Daddy go to Mrs Jones' pet shop. They buy a large aquarium with glass sides and a lid.
'You'll be able to keep several fish in there,' says Mrs Jones.

They also buy some gravel, a small net, a feeding ring and some fish food.

Setting up the aquarium

When they get home, Daddy puts the aquarium on a table out of the sunlight. Goldfish don't like too much warmth or bright light.

Next he spreads the gravel over the floor of the aquarium. He makes the gravel slope towards the front so that Susie will be able to see her goldfish clearly.

Then he puts some clean, rounded stones into the aquarium. Goldfish like somewhere to shelter or hide.

Filling the aquarium

Daddy puts a large cup inside the aquarium. He pours cold water into it so that it overflows. He continues pouring until the aquarium is nearly full. Filling an aquarium this way stops the gravel being washed away. Then Daddy takes the cup out.

Susie and Daddy must now wait until the water has risen to room temperature. Moving fish from warm water into cold (or the other way round) can kill them.

Common goldfish

Meanwhile, Susie and Daddy return to Mrs Jones' pet shop. They have decided to buy a few more goldfish and some water plants and water snails to put in the aquarium. Susie wonders which goldfish to choose – there are so many different kinds!

'It's best to start with common goldfish,' says Mrs Jones. 'They are the easiest to look after.'

At last, Susie chooses five goldfish, and they take everything home.

Water plants and snails

Daddy unwraps the water plants and lowers them into the aquarium. He anchors their roots with small stones.

'The plants will produce oxygen for the goldfish to breathe,' he explains. 'The goldfish can also feed on the plants or shelter beneath them.'

The snails climb up the aquarium's sides. The snails will help to keep the water clean by feeding on uneaten particles of food.

hornwort   Canadian pondweed   curly pondweed   eel grass

A new home

Daddy uses the net to move the fish into the aquarium. Moving them by hand could hurt them. He gently lowers them into the water, one by one.

The fish swim around the tank, exploring their new home.
'I think they like it,' says Susie happily.

Feeding the goldfish

Susie puts the feeding ring into the water, where it floats on the surface. Then she drops a pinch of fish food inside the ring. The ring stops the food drifting all over the aquarium. The fish dart towards the food and eat it hungrily. Soon there is none left.

'Never give fish more food than they can eat,' says Daddy, 'or they will become ill. One meal a day is all they need.'

In addition to dried fish food, goldfish will also eat water plants and chopped lettuce, as well as water fleas, freshwater shrimps, lice and worms. These can be bought frozen at a pet shop.

Cleaning the aquarium

It is very important to keep the aquarium clean. Daddy shows Susie how to remove particles of food and dirt with a glass tube called a pipette.

Daddy places a finger over one end of the pipette. He lowers the pipette into the water until the lower end is directly above a particle of food. Then he takes a finger off the top end and the food is sucked into the pipette. He lifts the pipette out of the water and washes it clean.
'How clever!' says Susie.

If the water in the aquarium becomes cloudy, it must be changed. The safest way of doing this is to fill buckets with cold tap water. Daddy leaves the buckets near the aquarium all day.

By late afternoon the water has reached room temperature. Daddy uses the net to lift the fish into the clean water, and empties the aquarium. He cleans the aquarium, then pours the clean water, and the fish, back inside.

Looking after goldfish

Goldfish need to be looked after carefully. They do not like sudden darkness or sudden bright lights. So at night, Daddy switches off the light in the lid a little before the room lights.

Goldfish also dislike sudden noises or vibrations.
'Never tap the side of the aquarium,' warns Daddy. 'It will give them a fright.'

Susie looks after her goldfish well. They grow bigger and bigger. Susie likes watching them swim among the stones and water plants.

'Perhaps one day, I will be able to keep tropical fish,' she says. 'They are often such beautiful colours.'
But Susie knows that tropical fish are also much more difficult to keep. And anyway, for the moment, she's quite happy with her six pretty goldfish.

Index

aquarium 4, 6, 8, 10, 16, 20, 22
common goldfish 12
feeding ring 6, 18, 24
fish food 6, 18, 20
tropical fish 26
water plants 12, 14, 18
water snails 12, 14
water temperature 10